GOD AT *In* WORK

Times of Loss

Text © 2000 by
Saint Meinrad Archabbey

Published by One Caring Place
Abbey Press
St. Meinrad, Indiana 47577

Library of Congress Catalog Number
00-101326

ISBN 0-87029-342-7

Printed in the United States of America

GOD AT
In WORK
Times
of Loss

Edited by R. Philip Etienne

Abbey Press
St. Meinrad, Indiana 47577

Introduction

While editing this book, a recurring message became evident: through life's grief and pain, God does not abandon us ... but is with us always, easing our losses. Even when we doubt God's presence and mercy, our Creator is at our side, bringing resolution and healing.

Everyone has been touched by the death of a loved one or has experienced some other significant loss in life ... that isn't especially unique. What is unique is how we each deal with our loss.

For instance, recently my aunt lost her husband to a heart attack—three days before her son's wedding. She had already lost a brother to cancer and her mother, my grandmother, remained in a nursing home, recovering from a close brush with death (Last Rites were administered just before Christmas).

When I arrived at the funeral home, I expected to find my aunt in a state of hysteria and misery. Instead, I found a strong, sensible woman who was holding up reasonably well under the circumstances. Along with the tears that flowed that evening, there were smiles, reassurances, and even laughter.

I marveled at her strength, trying to put myself in her place, wondering how I would deal with the loss she had faced. And then I looked at the people around her— her family ... my family. Faith has always been an integral part of this family. We've had many opportuni-

ties to thank God for many bless-
ings ... and have never failed to do
just that.

But this family, like others, has
also had its share of trying times.
And here we were again, relying on
faith to see us through. Looking at
the situation from that perspective,
it was not hard to recognize the
presence of God. For God is in all
of us ... and through us, God can
ease our pain. God can soothe and
encourage.

And with that presence of God
radiating within the room and
within me, I was able to understand
how my aunt was coping. And, in
turn, I was eased in my own grief.
God was truly at work.

—R. Philip Etienne

God comforts us in all our troubles so that we, in turn, may comfort others.

— II Corinthians 1:4

Where Is God When Bad Things Happen?

By Kay Talbot, Ph.D

Recently, I watched the movie *Forrest Gump* again and marveled at its message and connection with my life. Perhaps you, too, remember the last scene where Forrest visits the grave of his life-long love, Jenny, and says: *"I don't know if we each have a destiny, Jenny, or if we're all just floating around accidental-like, on a breeze—but I think maybe it's both. Maybe both happening at the same time."*

It's an age-old question: Do we arrive on Earth with our purpose and future unknown to us, yet pre-determined by God to unfold in ways known only to God? Are we sent here equipped with a God-given potential that we develop through our own actions? Or, as Forrest alludes, is life an even more complex combination of both destiny and personal choice?

One look at just a few of the marvels of our universe convinces me that, of course, there is a God. I have always believed that, pretty much without question. To me, the more difficult question that life eventually asks each of us actually forms the title of a book by Dr. Horace O. Duke: *Where Is God When Bad Things Happen?*

Where *is* God, we ask, when violence and evil wound and destroy God's people? We remember Job's plea: *"I cry out to you, O God, but you do not answer"* (Job 30: 20). Despite his righteousness and belief, Job suf-

fered greatly and without understanding.

In my own life, one certainly not
without sin and regrets, a day came
when the question of God's role
took an unforeseen and devastating
form. Where was God—what was
God doing that day, the day my
nine-year-old daughter, Leah, died
suddenly and unexpectedly, of an
unexplainable brain seizure?

God had been there when my
husband and I, unable to have our
own children, adopted Leah. I will
always remember the joy of that
moment. And God had been there,
too, the day her opthamologist told
me she would never be able to see—
and added, "Have you considered
not keeping her?" God was with me

as I regained my composure from this incredible assault, and responded, "No, we'll just work with whatever vision she ends up with." And God was there as Leah battled various physical conditions, never losing her joyful spirit. My prayers were answered as her vision grew and by third grade, she had become a voracious reader who wanted to grow up to be a writer.

But where was God when Leah had a sudden low blood sugar attack while at summer camp and was rushed to the hospital? Where was God the next day, when it appeared her body was recovering and then suddenly, without warning and despite all the doctors' efforts, she died? What was God doing? Did God take the day off?

I have learned much in searching for an answer to this question. Like all who grieve the death of a loved one, losing Leah ripped my heart open and exposed my soul to agony. Agony had once been only a word I knew that was used to describe great pain. Today, it has a meaning to me that I cannot describe to you in words. We can never totally understand another's pain.

Jesus gave us these words about agony, in Matthew 26, as he contemplated his future death: *"My soul is overwhelmed with sorrow to the point of death (v. 38)"*... *"My father, if it is not possible for this cup to be taken away unless I drink it, may your will be done (v. 42)."*

We read in Mark 15, that at his crucifixion, even Jesus questioned the whereabouts of God, crying out: *"My God, my God, why have you forsaken me (v. 34)?"* Jesus felt abandoned by God. How difficult it is for us to comprehend the agony of Creator and son at that moment, as God gave up his only son for the salvation of the world and God, too, became a bereaved parent.

Since Leah's death, I have heard many stories of grieving people who feel cut off from God. They are stories of spiritual crisis—what has been called "the dark night of the soul." One such story touched me deeply with its similarities to the story of Job. It is a mother's story of faith, tragedy, death, despair, and redemption.

In 1989, Donna Berger became the lone survivor of a highway accident when a tractor-trailer ran over her family's parked car, killing her husband and their three children, and leaving her critically burned. During long months in the hospital, Donna learned to rely on her faith and the inner strength it provided to find her way out of the vacuum of grief and confusion. Yet despite her faith, there came a time when she too felt abandoned by God.

It was at this lowest point that Donna came to realize that "to live a life of faith is very difficult, but to live without it is impossible." Donna began to feel stronger as she prayed for God to show her what she was supposed to do next.

Eventually she remarried, had three more children, and began to share her hard-won wisdom with others.

"Grief will not be denied," she says. "If you refuse to deal with it, you will never find peace. Grief is like an enormous boulder which must be ground into pebbles. There is no schedule. Each day you do what you can to chisel away at it. When you finally get down to the very last pebble, you put it in your pocket and carry it with you always and forever."

Today, like Donna, I carry a pebble which represents grief ground down to deep sadness. Leah's death changed my life in virtually every way. This singular experience led me to a new, unexpected purpose—

that of helping others to survive loss. In the early years of my grief, I never would have imagined I would leave the corporate world to return to graduate school and ultimately become a grief therapist and researcher. These accomplishments came much later, after I had worked through my own spiritual crisis.

During my darkest times, I held a bottle of pills in my hand, asking God why I should bother to go on living. The answer I heard was another question: How could you ever face Leah again if you kill yourself? She lived with such courage and joy. How can you do any less?

It was in this way that God was not only with me, but *in* me, sharing my pain and suffering. When we reach way down deep inside and listen to that small, still voice, we find the answer. Remember how God described himself to Moses? God said *"I am (Exodus 3:14)."* God did not say, "I was," or "I will be." God said "I am." I believe what God means by that is: "I am right here, inside you, experiencing life with you, feeling your pain and anger." In times of great need, when God seems to us to be absent, I believe that God's silence is not because God is not there. Rather, God's silence is the result of God's experiencing and sharing our overwhelming emotions.

At those times of deep despair, we are not able to speak but only to feel. God does not sit beside us in a detached way during these times.

God comforts us from the inside out, by feeling and absorbing our agony. Both Donna and I have learned, as it is written in Second Corinthians, that *"God comforts us in all our troubles so that we, in turn, may comfort others (1:4)."*

Our Creator gave us the awesome gift of free will. Having given that gift, God did not then back away to watch what we would do with it. Nor do I believe God directs our experiences like a puppeteer pulling strings. Rather, God enters into our experiences with us, creating each day anew. And God continually offers us renewed hope through modern-day examples of others who, like Job, have suffered greatly and been blessed to discover God's abiding love and healing presence.

Those who do not know how to weep with their whole heart don't know how to laugh either.

— Golda Meir

A Day God Dried My Tears

By Antoinette Bosco

The summer of 1994 was particularly difficult for me. Three-and-a-half years earlier, my beloved son, Peter, had died from suicide, at age 27, after an 11-year struggle with a faulty brain that took away his will to live.

I was still struggling with that pain two-and-a-half years later, when I got a phone call that again sheared my heart. I was called by a sheriff in Bigfork, Montana, telling me that my son, John, and his wife, Nancy, had been murdered in their home by an intruder.

I thought at first that I would die, too. But somehow I felt that I was being held by the Lord. Truly, I felt that my God was suffering with me, feeling my pain because I had lost children I so loved from unnatural causes—a chemical breakdown of brain cells in Peter's case, a gun in the hand of an amoral 18-year-old in the case of John and Nancy. Yet, even my faith could not take away the incessant torment of living with such heartbreaking loss.

In August of 1994, I had to prepare for the first anniversary of hearing the devastating news that my second son and his wife had been murdered. It was a Sunday, and instead of going to my regular parish church for Mass, I went to a church I loved in a nearby city because the Mass was at a more convenient hour that day for me.

We were going to have a first anniversary memorial for John and Nancy, and I had a crowd of family coming. I wanted to be home when they began arriving.

During the Mass, I kept praying to God intently, begging Him to take care of my boys, and to give me a sign that they were with him in Heaven. After receiving Communion, I was kneeling and thinking of my two sons, Peter and John, and then I asked them, "Was I right when I would tell you boys that 'Eye has not seen and ear has not heard what God has ready for those who love Him'?" I repeated it again, with my eyes closed.

I still feel in awe when I recall what happened at that moment. As I was voicing the words, the cantor began to sing, "Eye has not seen and ear has not heard..." a beautiful hymn I had never before heard! The tears came running down my cheeks. I just kept thanking the Lord for answering my question so quickly and in a way that was bound to get my attention. I could not have dreamed up a more perfect sign, or a more loving answer to my prayers.

I know others could say it was only by coincidence that the cantor was singing the very words that were on my silent tongue at that moment. But I know differently. This was another grace given to me by a loving God to let me know how truly He is there for us in our earthly pains. I know I was crying, but my cheeks weren't wet. God had dried my tears.

What we do for ourselves dies with us. What we do for others and the world remains and is immortal.

— Albert Pine

A Tree for Marjorie

By Nancy Stout

She died on May 23rd of this year. And it became clear to those around her, those close to her, that God continued to move within and through her to bless and to grace all that she touched, even in her last moments, and beyond.

Her husband expressed it best: "Marjorie's seven-day falling away was a love feast. The ties that connect our far-flung children were strengthened as they shared the discipline and the exhaustion of seeing her through. There was delight and laughter amidst our weeping as we reminisced.

"Most of the tears I've shed were triggered not by Marjorie, but by

unexpected stabs of joy and grati-
tude as I witnessed what was happening among us because of her," he
explained. "Ancient breaches between
Marjorie's sister and brother, and
between them and her, were sub-
stantially healed. (The sister, upon
witnessing the family at the memorial service and in Marjorie's house,
vowed to work hard to improve her
ties with her own child.)

"The hours and days were
thronged with happy chances and
spontaneities which were referred to
as 'serendipities,' but which each of
us came to acknowledge as
Providences—and to recognize that
Marjorie was somehow the source.
It was the fullest experience of clo-
sure—one provided by Marjorie her-
self. Her final gift to us."

But all of this was not the final gift from God—at work in this woman's life and in the lives of those connected to her. One day, not long after her death, I was in that state between being awake and being asleep, and I experienced a vision in which Marjorie came to me. She smiled her brightest smile, the one I had last seen just before her death. In this "visitation", she opened her arms wide, and she said, "My strength will be yours."

And I've been pondering that experience, those words, all summer. What do they mean? What do they promise to me? Marjorie had great strength, both in her living and her dying. And here she was, blessing me with that strength.

God worked in her life as she shared her joy, her love and affirmation with so many folks around her. God worked in her death to reconcile the estranged, to bring together friends and family and loved ones. God is working yet in my life, drawing from the tremendous impact she had on me as I traveled my own pathway through life.

Just today, as summer draws to a close, I went back to Marjorie's house. No one is there. Her husband is away until after Labor Day. But I went to visit the tree—planted in the back yard in memory of Marjorie. The tree honors her life, and it honors all new life. It is a symbol of hope, of growth, of continuity.

I entered the yard and closed the gate behind me. I went to the tree to touch it, then backed up several yards to sit. There was a calm there that I have been seeking recently. It was one of those moments when all seems in place and in order. It was a moment of incredible communion with the power and love of God.

It didn't last long—other noises in nearby yards quickly interrupted the quietness of the moment. But the peace—that remained. I was clearly within some invisible boundaries and protected by the Spirit of the Lord. Ah! I can see now ... this is the way God meant for it to be!

*C*omfort ye, comfort ye
my people says your God.

— Isaiah 40:1

God in the "Small Talk"

By Gordon W. Burton, M.Div.

"All she wanted to do was talk about death," said the white-haired gentleman seated across the table from me. This was his rationale for firing his last home-care nurse. My motives were quite clear. I wanted to know what she did wrong so that we did not make that same mistake.

I was new to the world of hospice care, and was desperately trying to find my niche as a hospice chaplain, stumbling along, trial and error, through what my supervisor would call "Precious Learning Experiences." These experiences were usually awkward, sometimes painful, but always instructive. I was trying very hard to pay attention.

"I know I'm dying," he continued. "I'm not in denial, like they said. I just don't want to talk about death all the time. There's lots better things to talk about. Like baseball."

I made up my mind right then to take every opportunity to talk baseball, or whatever he chose to talk about. On that day, I learned what it meant when people said, "Let the patient set the agenda."

Less than a year into the job, I was full of myself and my task. I was charged with assessing the spiritual needs of terminally ill persons and their families, and designing plans to meet those needs. I took that task seriously; I took myself very seriously.

I would write the *Spiritual Assessment*, a document which would eventually become a part of the ever-sacred *Patient Chart*. In it, I would comment on the depth of our conversations, or their superficiality. My thinking was that I had not done my job unless the greater part of the conversation was centered on serious matters: religious or spiritual issues, problems, concerns, unfinished business, and the like.

Somehow baseball games, fishing, cooking, the weather, and other topics didn't seem to count. They simply weren't serious enough.

The problem was, these latter topics were far easier to talk about, both for the patients and for me.

When I would assess a visit, and find it lacking in the sufficiently serious tone, I would ask whose fault it was. Was it the patient's fault? Were they in denial of their own mortality?

Or perhaps the fault was mine. Maybe I was uncomfortable with death and dying, and would avoid it by diverting into easier, softer, avenues of discussion.

Such was my thinking in relation to one of our newer patients, a young woman who was in a coma before she came to us. My visits were with her family. They had a strong faith in God, but no real church connection.

One of my goals was to be available to them in a pastoral way, to assist them in accessing their faith for comfort and support in this difficult time. Yet, each time I would visit, it seemed we talked about everything except what was happening with their daughter and their feelings about it.

When the talk turned in the direction of their daughter's impending death, they veered quickly away just as the tears began to form, venturing instead into such difficult territory as politics, the local professional football team, hobbies, my children's experience at college, if it was time to hunt mushrooms, and on and on, all over the map. We went everywhere but back to their feelings about God and faith, and illness, and death.

Their daughter died, regardless of how little we talked about it. The family asked me to conduct the funeral. I visited the funeral home to pay my respects and to talk with them about the service.

They were appropriately grieving, talking about their daughter's life and death and faith and in her place with God. "Finally," I thought, "some quality spiritual time."

As I was preparing to leave, one of the patient's sisters took me aside to express her thanks for the hospice team and the help given in the last weeks of her sister's life. She wanted especially to thank me for helping her and her parents, for being willing to visit and talk "normally" with them.

My expression must have betrayed my question. Before I could ask, she explained that I had been the only one who talked about things other than her sister's illness and death. Following one of my visits, her parents told her how nice it was to be able to talk about normal things, about life.

In *my* mind, I had failed them by not properly addressing weighty matters. In *their* minds, I had touched them deeply, giving them something they very much wanted and needed—a sense of normalcy in the midst of their pain. Her exact words were: "They felt comforted when you left. You gave them a chance to relax and look at life."

Isaiah 40:1 came to my mind: "Comfort ye, comfort ye my people says your God." This is at least part of what I was able to be about, bringing comfort to God's people.

Is it possible that one of the ways to comfort others is with the normal, even superficial, conversations, the willingness to let go of the more weighty matters for a time and look at some of the more trivial things of life? Can a sense of the superficial, the mundane, and even the silly, be comforting, healthy, even holy?

Jesus himself even addressed the issue when he talked of faithfulness in the small things. "Whoever can be trusted with very little can also be trusted with much..." (*Luke*

16:10a). The lesson for me is clear: Spirituality can be found anywhere and everywhere, even and perhaps especially, in the little things, in the "small talk."

The comfort of God comes in many ways, shapes, and sizes, and most often, it seems, when we aren't even looking for it.

This story first appeared in *The Journal of Pastoral Care*, Fall 1999, Vol. 353, No. 3, and is reprinted with the kind permission of the publisher.

Every exit is an entrance somewhere else.

— Tom Stoppard

Saints Be Praised!
By Ray Mathews

My wife and I had already been blessed with a beautiful baby girl, and were looking forward to the birth of our second child.

At that time of young dreams and high hopes, however, there was no way we could have anticipated that our new baby would be born prematurely. We were caught completely off-guard when he arrived six weeks early.

Our doctor immediately prepared us for the reality that the outlook was not too hopeful. Many of today's medical advances had not yet been achieved back then. As it turned out, our doctor was correct in his concern. Our newborn baby boy lived only one day and we were overcome by a deep and sudden sense of loss.

It was indeed a time of sadness for us and our families. We received an outpouring of cards and letters from relatives and friends who were most generous in their heartfelt expressions of sympathy and condolences. However, among the many people who expressed their thoughts and feelings, there was one friend at the office who took me completely by surprise.

Apparently, the usual and familiar words of sympathy were not on his mind or in his heart. Wearing one of his most cheerful Irish smiles, and extending his hand to me in friendship, he said most sincerely and enthusiastically, "Congratulations! You have a saint in heaven!"

What a blessing it was to hear those uplifting words of a friend whose unwavering faith strengthened mine and made the healing a little easier.

*T*he great art of life is sensation, to feel that we exist, even in pain.

— Lord Byron

Respecting the Pieces

By Rev. Dr. Richard B. Gilbert

One of my favorite skits from the famous comedian, Jonathan Winters, involved him looking around in an attic and finding objects that we would look at and wonder, "Why would anyone save that junk?" But he would look at an object and see a story, a feeling, a memory. He saw an attic full of precious things, while we see junk, pieces, the scattering.

We know what it feels like to have our lives shattered and scattered ... pieces. An aging parent dies after a lingering battle with cancer. A child is ripped from us through miscarriage. A drunk driver plows into our son's car. A kid is wiped out because of a stray bullet: wrong person, wrong place, wrong time.

Loss rips us to shreds, and can leave us feeling abandoned, disheartened and maybe unable to believe. The faith that walks with us through our sorrow often seems dark, bleak, and filled with despair. Loss is never neat and tidy, and it is hard to believe faith is at work when life is a pile of rubble.

When grieving, we often believe the challenge is to put the pieces together and get on with our lives. Faith respects the pieces and values the stories, feelings, and memories in each shattered experience. Faith says that everything within and around us is valuable, even when we believe otherwise.

Holy Mother Mary knew what it was to feel grief. Her life as a parent was a constant struggle, facing the world's unwillingness to welcome and embrace the gifts of her Son. She, too, was a bereaved mother. She saw a life of pieces and pondered them all in her heart.

Pondering. That's the gift of faith that meets us in our pieces. Pondering is not the picking up of the pieces and getting things back to the way they were. Faith is never about going backwards. Faith is about the God who meets us in the pieces. When you are grieving, feeling shattered to pieces, wandering through the attics of memories and stories, meet God there. God awaits you. Ponder.

*O*ne of the illusions of life is that the present hour is not the critical, decisive hour. Write on your heart that every hour is the best day of the year.

— Emerson

Finding God in Times of Loss

By Ruth Ellen Hasser

We were riding up the slope on a ski lift for the first run of the day, our legs dangling freely over fresh powder and evergreen treetops. The air was crisp, the sky a deep blue, and the majesty of the mountains surrounded us on every side. My friend, a self-proclaimed atheist, drew in a breath and quietly muttered in awe, "It's hard not to believe in God at a time like this!"

Years later, in the far less majestic surroundings of a sterile hospital room, another friend, Joan, watched her father die a slow and painful death. Here was a man who worked hard all his life, loved his family well, and never intentionally hurt a soul. Now, he hovered somewhere between life and death, struggling for four long months. Joan's heart was breaking as she helplessly watched her father's diminishment. She ached at his undeserved pain, and at her own loss of the Daddy she loved so deeply. Her prayers for either his healing or quick and peaceful death apparently unanswered, she wondered, "Where is God in all of this?"

Anyone who has experienced life comes to know the pain of loss, both great and small. From those earliest moments of emerging out of the warm, comfortable place of our mothers' wombs, to those final moments of death, we each know loss intimately. As spiritual beings, we look for answers to our questions about the meaning of such losses, and we often discover that the deeper our pain, the fewer the answers we easily find. Believing in God is much easier in the majestic mountains than in the desert valleys.

In the days and weeks following my father's sudden death, God cared for me in immeasurable ways. The cards, prayers, flowers, and hugs from friends; the delicious meals cooked lovingly for me on those days I would have otherwise eaten cold cereal for dinner; the understanding of office colleagues at my frequent forgetfulness; all were evidence of God's tender mercies in my life. At the time, I was just "getting by." Looking back, God's love is crystal clear.

It is often the experience of people of faith that, although they may not recognize it at the time, God was there for them in their time of need. Shortly after *her* father died, Joan was able to reflect and notice that, though incredibly difficult, those final months with him had provided her and her family with many graces.

The time together allowed them to "say once more how much we loved him, and to thank him for what he taught us. Although he was suffering, we were still able to hold his hand." She was graced with an awareness of the sacrament of time. Joan found that by embracing the mystery of his dying, and releasing her father into God's care, she was able to know a peace that "answers" alone cannot give.

So, too, with each of us. God's love and grace is available to us each moment of each day, in both our magnificent mountains and in our driest desert valleys. Sometimes, all we need is a quiet moment of prayer to recall that grace. Other times, it may come to us in the touch of a hand, the scent of fresh bed linens, the sight of the sky at daybreak, or in the loving goodbye between parent and child. We are never forgotten or forsaken. We have been lovingly carved into the palm of God's hand.

*I*t is hard to have patience with people who say "There is no death" or "Death doesn't matter." There is death. And whatever is matters. And whatever happens has consequences, and it and they are irrevocable and irreversible. You might as well say that birth doesn't matter.

— C.S. Lewis

Forgiving God

By Lorri Malone

I was pregnant once. I was jubilant, excited and ecstatic. And then suddenly I wasn't pregnant. I was hurt, disappointed and angry.

I was especially angry at God.

Sure, I could have directed my anger at all of those well-intentioned, but ultimately tactless, folks who felt compelled to comment on my unfortunate miscarriage:

"At least you weren't very far along." I was far along enough to know my husband and I had created a life.

"It's a good thing, really. There was probably something wrong with the baby."

Do not underestimate my potential to care for a child who is born less than perfect.

"At least you didn't carry for nine months and give birth to a stillborn." The two situations are not comparable at all. My heartache deserved to be acknowledged in and of itself.

"Just get pregnant again real soon and you'll feel better." The birth of another child would not just magically erase the pain of this loss.

"If you had just lost weight/gotten rid of your cat/eaten right/slept more/been less stressed/quit working/stopped exercising/kept quiet until the end of the first trimester/cut out caffeine, this never would have happened." My miscarriage happened because

of medical causes that were beyond my or my doctor's control.

"I know how you feel." No, you don't, and I hope you never do.

While I was annoyed and sometimes hurt by many of the remarks others made, I tried to appreciate their attempts to comfort. But long after the miscarriage was over and things were back to the way they had been before the pregnancy, I could still feel this underlying anger that made me feel guilty. I tried to pinpoint it. Was I angry at my husband for getting me pregnant? No, that wasn't it.

After much soul-searching, I came to the conclusion that I was mad at God. Though it may seem arrogant on my part, I felt that God had put me and my husband through a gut-wrenching disappointment that we didn't deserve. The Lord outfitted me with this complicated female body. It is God who controls destiny, fate. If God gets credit for creating, then I figured surely God also deserves credit for destroying. With that newfound perspective, I embraced my anger and let it flow.

But you know, in my heart I love God. Just as with a beloved family member who angers and disappoints, I knew I had to get past those feelings and start to forgive. I have to accept God's plan and actions. I just don't always have to like them, however. It took time for me to accept my feelings of anger and even more time for me to let go of them. But I did. And eventually I forgave God.

We are blessed today with a beautiful, healthy, and perfect baby boy. A peace offering from above perhaps? Maybe God is at work healing my once-broken heart and teaching me the ultimate virtue of forgiveness.

*A*lthough the world is full of suffering, it is full also of the overcoming of it.

—Helen Keller

Resurrection

By Fr. Joe Weigman

I love kids. Since as a priest I will not have children of my own, a special part of my ministry has been visiting the parish grade school. It was on one such visit, during Holy Week, when one of the second-graders asked me, "What's so *good* about Good Friday?"

It's a valid question. Certainly, Good Friday does not seem good at all when we focus only on the death of Jesus. Good Friday gets better, though, when we celebrate Easter Sunday. The Easter celebration reminds us that Jesus' death leads to resurrection, new life.

Resurrection is what awaits us after *we* die, too; however, we do not have to wait for physical death to experience the new life of resurrection. Death is a not uncommon part of life—goodbyes that we have to say to friends who move away, marriages that come to an end, the loss of a certain way of life. The most significant death I have experienced is the loss of the understanding of myself as healthy. Death, of course, is never the end of the story.

While I was on retreat, just before my ordination to the transitional diaconate, eight months before ordination to the priesthood, I often experienced sharp pains in my legs. One day, after a long walk, I began to stumble. Actually, I had had similar experiences in previous months, but they were easy to dismiss because they were sporadic and never very dramatic. The time had come when I could no longer ignore what I was experiencing.

After a few months of various tests and procedures, I was diagnosed by a neurologist as having multiple sclerosis. It seemed as if God was playing a joke on me: after years of questioning my call to priesthood, I was diagnosed with a chronic disease less than three months before my ordination to priesthood.

My first reaction to the diagnosis was to continue to think of myself as healthy. I guess I figured that if I ignored MS, like I ignored its first symptoms, it would disappear. Besides, I did not want a bunch of attention or sympathy from the other guys in the seminary. My diagnosis was, initially, a personal affair.

Fortunately, when the reality of having a disease hit, I learned that I did not have to go through my loss alone. I rediscovered the love and support of my family, for example. I was not surprised by their reaction, but I was somewhat unprepared for the outpouring of love and support shown me by the seminary community. While I had always considered myself *giving* life to the community, I was now *receiving* life from the community—through kind words, through generous deeds, through constant prayer. Slowly, the death of my diagnosis was evolving into a resurrection. By the end of the school year, I knew that the trust I had come to have in others was the same kind of trust I needed to have in God.

Now that I have lived with multiple sclerosis for several years, I have experienced the love and support of many other people, including the people in the parish communities I have served. Even with the wonderful people the Lord has sent into my life, I can still sometimes doubt that God always was and always will be with me.

Mostly, though, I live with a new confidence in God's love and care for me. No, I am not completely healthy; but when others show me a little bit of what God's love looks like, even being a person with physical disabilities is *good*.

Life is about not knowing, having to change, taking the moment and making the best of it, without knowing what's going to happen next. Delicious ambiguity.

— Gilda Radner

Losing Your Husband

By Karen Katafiasz

The book club mailing, addressed to my late husband, was meant for former members. "What can we do to get you back?" asked the pleading cartoon figure on the front. I had to smile at the question's sad irony. *I wish I knew*, I thought. Even though John had died years before, such words could still trigger strong feelings.

Few events can affect a married woman so profoundly and change every part of her life so drastically as the death of her husband. For me, its impact was like that of a devastating earthquake. The life we had together was ripped apart, pieces of my existence crumbled around me, the world became unsafe and unsteady. And, like a massive earth-quake, it produced a relentless series of aftershocks that were powerful and disruptive.

I wondered if I'd ever recover from the trauma of losing my husband. Days seemed weighed down by a sense of hopelessness. But as difficult as this time was, the belief that I could hold on, that I could find comfort, that I could get through sustained me ... and saved me.

"No one ever told me that grief felt so like fear," C.S. Lewis wrote after the death of his beloved wife, Joy. It was also, at times, like "being mildly drunk, or concussed," he added. And sometimes, he said, it was even "laziness."

Grief is all that and more: shock, denial, anger, depression, despair, guilt, confusion, bitterness, regret. And because the marriage relationship is so encompassing, intricate, and deep, one's emotions are understandably complex and especially intense.

At first, I was a little numb and had a sense of unreality. At the same time, I questioned how this could be numbness when I was feeling so much pain—until the numbness started to wear off and I realized the pain really can get worse.

A particularly harsh part of losing my husband was that there were so many practical matters, of all types and degrees of importance, that demanded my attention, just when I was emotionally devastated. And the one person with whom I usually discussed and shared these kinds of concerns was gone. I started learning very quickly all that it meant to be without my husband.

Funeral and burial arrangements; thank-you notes; the will; insurance; name changes on bank accounts and credit cards, on house and car titles; cleaning out his closet—these tasks seemed to require more attention and energy than I could summon. But I did what had to be done and postponed what I could.

About a year after John died, I felt myself at a deeper level of pain—the early protective numbness had worn off—and my grieving seemed stuck there. I joined a support group for widowed persons, where we told our stories and shared an understanding that was deeper than the words we spoke. Spending time with other widows moved me along in the grieving process, making all the difference.

The loneliness at times seemed (and still seems, at times) so crushing it was hardly bearable. After all, I lost the most important person in my life—my friend, companion, confidant, supporter, helper. Other people couldn't take his place or make the awful loneliness vanish. But their presence could bring consolation. I took time to be with persons I was comfortable with, persons I could talk to, persons I could hug.

Great loss can challenge your spiritual beliefs. I found myself angry with God, feeling abandoned, and even punished. The faith that used to give me consolation and strength seemed ineffectual, hollow. But I grew to realize I didn't have to go through this spiritual dark night alone. There were (and are) pastoral ministers and counselors who can help deal with bereavement.

Great loss can also jar you into a deeper awareness of what's truly important in life. I let my pain make me more compassionate, understanding, and loving. It has taught me how not to take for granted life's wonder and goodness.

I cherish the relationship that my husband and I shared. His love, his presence, changed me and left me a richer, better person. The differences he made in my life are part of his legacy, and I carry that with me always.

During the worst periods of my grieving, I began to doubt that life would ever seem joyful and worthwhile again. But it did. Finally one day, I realized that my laughter was different; I actually felt happy, and even had a sense of peace. Life won't ever be the same though, and neither will I.

There may always be a small, empty place within me ... a wound that never heals. But I value it. It's God's way of sustaining my connection to the man who was so significant in my life.

"I once heard an undoubtedly good-intentioned minister say to a grieving widow, 'Too many tears send the message that we doubt the resurrection of the dead.' I didn't correct him (he had, after all, been in the ministry before I was even born) but I couldn't help thinking how off track he was. Jesus' mourning of his friend Lazarus gave birth to tears even though he knew for a fact that in a matter of minutes Lazarus would be alive, set free from the darkness of the bonds of the tomb. And so perhaps the tears didn't speak of doubt of the resurrection of the dead, but acknowledgement of the toll it takes on the living."

—Fr. Alaric Lewis, O.S.B.

Home

By Fr. Alaric Lewis, O.S.B.

My mother died on a Saturday. Dad had been gone all night, but we really didn't think much of that because he often spent the night with Mom when she was in the hospital. It was during the *Bugs Bunny/Road Runner Hour* that he walked through the door, his face a mask of defeat. He turned off the television (I remember being upset about this) and broke the news.

The next few hours was a succession of tangible and vocal pain that even now, even for the nothing-is-beyond-reflection me, is still a bit too much to deal with. But after all of this, Dad decided that we had to continue doing what we did, that only some semblance of normalcy could allow us to endure the torturous chaos that swirled about us. And so, every Saturday without fail, we always went uptown to Deck's Drugstore, for a chocolate milkshake, and this Saturday would be no different.

But things were different. As I walked into Deck's, I felt as if I had never been there before. The familiarity of this treasured place had disappeared. Once a place of happiness and warmth, it now seemed cold, sterile, unforgiving. News of the death had reached the drugstore before we had, and my Dad, brother, and I were met by the eyes of patrons, red from crying.

Why were they crying, I wondered; it was my mother, not theirs, and Dad told us that we had to be brave, and so I couldn't cry. One woman, her lace handkerchief pressed to her mouth, muttered, "Those poor children," and I wanted to scream, to smash all the collectible Coke bottles that lined the antique back-piece of the counter. Even the milkshake, what had been the very nectar of my youth, tasted bitter and foul. I wanted to spit it out. I wanted to cry and scream. I wanted to smack those pitying faces with their red eyes.

All of this was in me, but it would not, could not, come out. I was in a foreign place, among people who, despite their familiar faces, were strangers, adversaries. I would not allow this place, these people, to really see me. I stayed very close to my father's side until we could leave it all.

Upon returning to our home, I began running around to different places. I ran down to the basement, and allowed the cool damp air to become a part of my own fractured breathing. I ran to my parents' bedroom and swore that I could smell her on her pillow, although her head hadn't laid there in a while. I ran to the back yard, running around the bases where my brother played ball with his friends, but where they said I was too small to play, run along. And I ran to my tree, to the best climbing tree I had ever encountered anywhere.

I climbed as high as I could,
above it all—above the death, above
the sadness, above the relatives,
above the neighbors and their hams
and their casseroles. I climbed and
was enveloped in the leafy familiarity of my tree. And as I sat as high as
I dared, surrounded by the loving
embrace of her branches, I began to
weep. I wept for it all: for the fact
that I wouldn't see her again; for the
injustice of it; for the sheer hatred
and anger at a world that would do
this to me.

The feelings that were within
me and a part of me, that I would
not, could not, show in that drugstore or, later, in the funeral home
or the church or the cemetery, I
could show here. I could cry and
scream and hit the trunk of that

tree as hard as I was able, as if I was hitting her. And I could do all of this, show all of this, because I was home.

And I know now that home is not a house. It is not a quaint collo-quialism easily cross-stitched and put on a pillow not to be really used as a pillow at all. Home is the place where you can be yourself, where you don't have to worry about the judgments and stares and disap-proval of people. Home is where you can cry and scream, by God, if that's what your soul is calling for.

And home is filled with people who might not always understand, who might want to cry and scream at different times than you do, but who allow you to be who you are, and none other. And this realization, this coming home, could have come from none other than our ultimate destination, the God of the living who can speak even through death.

God at Work Series

- *God at Work…
  in Times of Loss.* #20096

- *God at Work…
  in Times of Trouble.* #20095

- *God at Work…
  Through the Voices of
  Children.* #20097

Available at your favorite bookstore
or gift shop, or directly from:
One Caring Place, Abbey Press,
St. Meinrad, IN 47577
(800) 325-2511
www.onecaringplace.com